FOR BOYS AND GIRLS AGE 10 & UP

STOP!
· Just For Kids ·

FOR KIDS WITH SEXUAL TOUCHING PROBLEMS
BY KIDS WITH SEXUAL TOUCHING PROBLEMS

Adapted From The Original Writings By
Terri Allred, M.T.S. and Gary Burns, M.S.

Safer Society Press

PO BOX 340 · BRANDON, VERMONT 05733 · (802) 247-3132

STOP! Just For Kids
Copyright © 1997
Terri Allred and Gary Burns
Second printing 1999

Design, Illustration, and Typesetting: Barbara Poeter, Pittsford, Vermont

Printing: Whitman Communications, Inc., Lebanon, New Hampshire

Copies of this book may be ordered from:
THE SAFER SOCIETY PRESS
PO Box 340
Brandon, VT 05733-0340
(802) 247-4233

$15.00 per copy

ISBN: 1-884444-37-7

THANKS

*T*HIS IS WHERE *we get to thank the people who helped us write this book. We want to thank Mr. Burns, our teacher, for taking his time to teach us and help us write this book. We want to thank Ms. Allred, our therapist, for helping us in our treatment and supporting us. They both put in a lot of effort and time, rushing through meals and sitting in groups with us.*

We would like to thank Hermitage Hall and the community for allowing us to be in treatment to work on our problems.

We thank Lisa Muniz and Daniel Hilliker for typing our book.

4

A special thanks goes to our parents, families, case workers, and Bears unit staff for supporting us through our treatment.

WHAT IS IN THIS BOOK

9

STOP! JUST FOR KIDS

WELCOME TO OUR BOOK

*W*E ARE THE *Good News Bears. We are kids, just like you, who have sexual touching problems. Before we get started, we have a couple of things we would like you to know. We are writing this book because we broke our families' and communities' trust by hurting others in a sexual way. We hope that our book will help other kids with sexual touching problems, before they hurt someone or commit a sexual offense. We are awfully sorry for hurting people. We are happy to have treatment to help us with our problems. Sometimes working on our problems is hard, but we know it is worth it, if we can keep from hurting ourselves or anyone else.*

In our book we will be talking a lot about therapists. They are really cool people who help us with our problems. Our therapist is a woman, so in the book we use female pronouns like "she" or "her" to describe a therapist. We know that men can be good therapists too. We just thought it would be less confusing this way.

We have included a new word list at the beginning of the book. We think it would be a good idea for you to read it first, so that you will understand the words we use. This is how we did it when we were learning. We also underlined each new word the first time we used it in the book.

8

NEW WORDS LIST

✓ **Accountable** — Taking responsibility for your behavior.

✓ **Anger** — When you feel really mad and don't like what happened.

✓ **Assertive** — Standing up for yourself and saying what you want without hurting others.

Bestiality — Doing sexual things with animals.

✓ **Bribe** — Making promises to trade one thing for another thing you want. An example of this would be to give your little sister candy so that she won't tell on you.

Child Sexual Abuse — An older person doing sexual things with someone not old enough to say it is okay.

Coercion — To make someone do things, or let you do things to them, that they don't want to.

Confused — To not understand or feel mixed up.

Conscience — A voice inside of you that tells you right from wrong, and how to make good choices.

Consent — Permission.

N E W   W O R D S

✓ **Consequences** — The results of your behavior.

✓ **Deny** — To say something didn't happen when you know it did.

✓ **Empathy** — To understand and care about the thoughts and feelings of someone else.

Exhibitionism — When you show your private parts to somebody else.

Fantasy — Thoughts about being sexual; like a daydream.

✓ **Feeling** — An emotion that happens from the neck down; like sad, mad, worried, or happy.

✓ **Fondle** — To touch someone's private parts without their permission. This is a sexual offense.

✓ **Force** — Physically make others do things they do not want to do.

✓ **Frottage** — To rub your hands or private parts against someone without their permission. This is a sexual offense.

✓ **Frustration** — To feel like nothing is going right.

N E W W O R D S

Groom — To set others up so you can sexually offend them.

Guilt — Feeling bad about what you did.

Honesty — Truth; the truth, the whole truth, and nothing but the truth.

Hopeless — Feeling like everything is bad or wrong and nothing or no one can make it better.

Illegal — Something that is not allowed by the law.

Inside Blocks — "Walls" that you make up in your heart and head that remind you to make good choices, like to not sexually offend.

Intimidate — Saying or doing things to scare others.

Jealous — To want something that someone else has, like a new toy or your mom's attention.

Legal — Something that is allowed by the law.

Legal Age of Consent — The age it is legal to give permission to do something sexually.

N E W   W O R D S

Manipulate — Tricking others into doing things you want them to do.

Masturbate — To touch your own private parts.

Minimize — To make something sound not important.

Outside Block — "Walls" that you place outside of you to stop you from sexually offending, like making sure you are not alone with little kids.

Personal Space — The amount of space that people need around them to feel comfortable.

16

Positive Attention — Attention you get for doing good things.

Private Parts — The parts of your body that are covered by a swimsuit.

Problem Solving — Working things out when there is a problem.

Rape — Using coercion or force to make someone have sex. This is a sexual offense.

Rationalize — To make up reasons for what you did to take the blame off of you.

17

N E W   W O R D S

Respect — To think and care about how others feel.

Responsible — Taking credit or blame for your thoughts and behavior.

Revenge — To hurt or "get back" at someone for something they did to you.

Sadness — To be unhappy.

Sexual Abuse — Sexual behavior that harms another or is illegal, like having sex without consent.

Sexual Arousal — Exciting or tingling urges in your private parts that sometimes happen with sexual thoughts.

Sexual Offense — A sexual action that hurts another person and is against the law.

Sexual Offense Cycle — The steps of thoughts, feelings, and behaviors leading up to doing a sexual offense.

Sexual Touching Problem — A problem kids have who want to touch or hurt others sexually or do sexual things with others without their permission.

Sexuality — All the things that have to do with having sexual parts, being a sexual person, and being sexual with others.

Sexually Transmitted Diseases — Sicknesses you can get when you do sexual things with people who already have these sicknesses.

Support System — The group of people who help you with your problems.

Therapist — A person trained to help you with your problems.

Thinking Problems — Thoughts that make it easier to sexually offend. Some examples of thinking problems are: minimizing, denying, or rationalizing.

Thought — Something that happens from the neck up. The things that you say to yourself in your mind or head.

Threat — Telling others bad things will happen if they do not do what you want.

Trigger — Something that makes it easier for a kid to start thinking or feeling like hurting someone sexually.

N E W   W O R D S

Trust — When you feel safe around someone.

Victim — Someone who is hurt by others.

Voyeurism — Being sneaky and watching others be naked or have sex without their consent. This is a sexual offense.

Warning Signs — Things we teach ourselves about how to tell when our sexual offense cycle is about to happen.

CHAPTER 1

The First Big Step: HONESTY!

23

WHY IS **_HONESTY_** first? Honesty is when you tell the truth. If you aren't honest, then people can't help you. It's like going to the doctor with a stomach ache and telling her your leg hurts. She can't help solve the problem unless you are honest with her.

And ... we can't stop our behavior unless we are honest with ourselves and others about what we did.

24

Being honest is not always easy. This is because:

- We are afraid others will not believe us.

- We are embarrassed.

- We are afraid we will get in trouble.

- We are afraid people will not like us.

- We are afraid that, if we tell the truth, people will know we have a problem.

Here are some of the reasons it is important to be honest:

Telling the truth may help make you feel better. We felt better when we were honest because:

- Someone finally understood our confusing <u>feelings</u>.

- Our <u>therapist</u> listened to us without laughing.

- Our families learned how to help us.

Telling the truth helps others learn how to help you with your problems.

Telling the truth helps other children learn to be honest about their problems.

28

Telling the truth helps you learn how you have hurt others so that you can learn how to stop.

When you tell the truth and admit what happened, you are being accountable. This means that you are taking responsibility for your behavior.

It is respectful to others and yourself to be honest.

30

One way that you can be honest is to tell what happened and how you feel. This means you have to tell everything, even the hardest stuff.

Sometimes, it's hard to be honest, especially when you haven't been telling the truth for a long time. But remember: your family and therapist can help you only if they know what the problem is.

One of the reasons we wrote this book is to show other kids that it is okay to be honest about your worries and <u>sexual</u> <u>touching</u> <u>problems</u>. It was hard for us to be honest and we were scared, but being honest was the first step to learning better ways to solve our problems.

Can you think of two people who you can be honest with about your sexual touching problems? Who are they? What will you tell them?

REMEMBER — the truth, the whole truth, and nothing but the truth!

32

CHAPTER 2

What Happened To Us and What We Did

WE DECIDED TO talk about *what happened to us* and *what we did to others* together, because sometimes they are hard to separate; sorta like peanut butter and jelly.

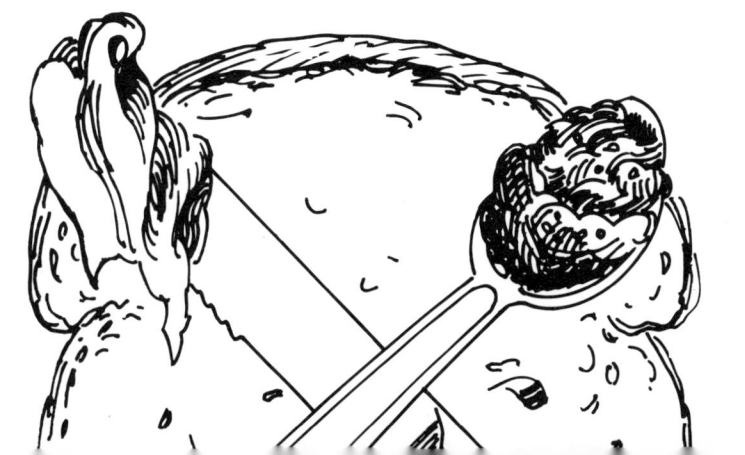

Some kids who touch others in a sexual way without their permission had scary or hurtful things happen to them.

When scary things happened that hurt them, they were <u>victims</u>.

But even if someone hurt them, it isn't okay for them to hurt someone else.

36

Kids with sexual touching problems hurt others by doing sexual things without <u>consent</u>, tricking or <u>manipulating</u> others, or taking advantage of people who don't understand about sex.

This does not mean that kids with sexual touching problems are bad. It means the things that happened to them or the things they did are wrong.

38

Sometimes we confuse *hurting others* and *being hurt* because:

- When we talk about what we did, it makes us think about what happened to us.

- When we talk about what happened to us, we sometimes want to hurt other people.

When bad things happen, we have a lot of <u>confused</u> <u>thoughts</u> and feelings.

40

We sometimes act out these thoughts and feelings. Sometimes we don't make good choices when we try to get these confused thoughts and feelings out.

Children who have been hurt and who have hurt others have a lot of feelings. Here are some of the feelings they share.

- Anger.
- Sadness.
- Guilt.
- Hopelessness.

42

Sometimes kids hurt others when they feel bad. One way that kids can hurt others is to do sexual things to them.

Sometimes we don't like to talk about the sexual things we do to hurt others or the things people did to hurt us. This is because we are:

- <u>Denying</u> our problems and pretending they aren't there.
- Trying to keep people from holding us accountable for what we did.
- Thinking only of ourselves.
- Shy or embarrassed.
- Worried about what other people will think of us.

44

We need to talk about these things so that:

- We won't hurt others.

- We can realize we are not the only kid who has this problem.

- We can learn about being responsible for our behavior.

- We won't keep it locked up inside.

Sometimes it is easier to blame other people for what we do. Then we don't have to admit when we do things that are wrong and hurt others.

46

Just because someone may have hurt you does not give you the right to hurt others.

It was wrong when you were hurt
and
it is wrong to hurt others!

48

STOP! JUST FOR KIDS

CHAPTER 3

Sexual Touching Problems

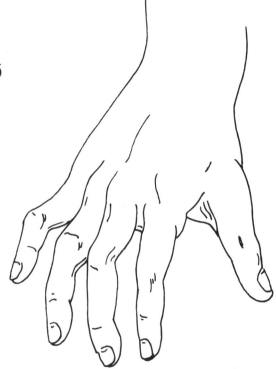

B efore we can **STOP** our sexual touching problems, we need to know what those problems *are.*

50

There are some very important words we need to know before we can understand our sexual touching problems.

When you ask someone to do something sexual with you, that person has to say it is OK. This is called consent.

Consent means permission, *but* this means the person has to be old enough and able to understand what you are asking permission to do or say.

It doesn't count if they do what you want them to because they are afraid you won't like them if they don't. It also doesn't count if they do what you want them to because they don't have a choice.

52

There are different ways that kids with sexual touching problems make other kids be sexual or do sexual things. Here are some of those ways.

Coercion means <u>force</u>, <u>threats</u>, <u>bribes</u>, manipulation, or <u>intimidation</u> to get others to do what you want.

Force means physically making others do things.

54

Threats means telling others bad things will happen to them if they don't do what you want them to.

Bribes means giving others presents or money so that  they will do sexual things with you or keep a secret about sexual things.

Manipulation means tricking others into doing things by using their feelings.

55

Intimidation means saying or doing things to scare others so they will do what you want them to do, sorta like being a bully!

When you use one of these types of coercion to get someone to do something sexual with you, it is called <u>sexual</u> <u>abuse</u>.

56

Different states have different laws about how people should treat each other.

Legal behavior is something that is allowed by law.

Illegal behavior is something that is *not* allowed by law.

SEXUAL ABUSE is ILLEGAL in all states!

Now that we understand the difference between consent and coercion, legal and illegal behavior, it will be easier to understand <u>sexual</u> <u>offenses</u>.

These are some sexual offenses:

> Sexual abuse is having sex without consent.

> <u>Rape</u> is using coercion to get someone to have sex.

> <u>Child</u> <u>sexual</u> <u>abuse</u> is having sex with someone under the <u>legal</u> <u>age</u> <u>of</u> <u>consent</u>.

58

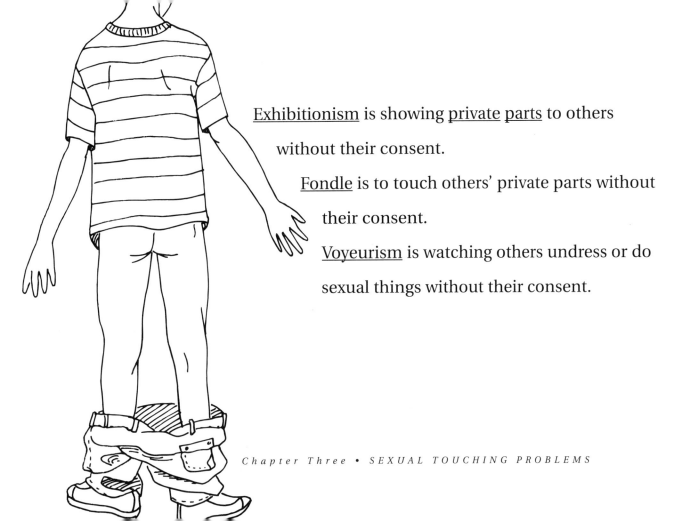

<u>Exhibitionism</u> is showing <u>private</u> <u>parts</u> to others without their consent.

<u>Fondle</u> is to touch others' private parts without their consent.

<u>Voyeurism</u> is watching others undress or do sexual things without their consent.

<u>Frottage</u> is rubbing your private parts against someone without their consent.

<u>Bestiality</u> is doing sexual things with an animal.

REMEMBER! ANIMALS CANNOT GIVE CONSENT!

60

These things are against the law and they hurt others.

When kids with sexual touching problems make bad choices there are <u>consequences</u> or things that happen because of what they do.

Here are some ways your sexual touching problems may affect you and others …

62

When you act on your sexual touching problems you AFFECT OTHERS:

- You hurt others.

- You make others feel unsafe.

- You may cause physical damage.

- You make others feel bad about themselves.

- You make others feel like you did if someone hurt you in a sexual way.

Your sexual touching problems can cause FAMILY PROBLEMS:

- You may not be allowed to see all of your family.

- Your family and people you care about may treat you differently.

- Your family may be very worried or feel like they don't know how to help you.

- You may not be allowed to live at home if you sexually abused a brother or sister.

64

Your sexual touching problems can cause SCHOOL PROBLEMS:

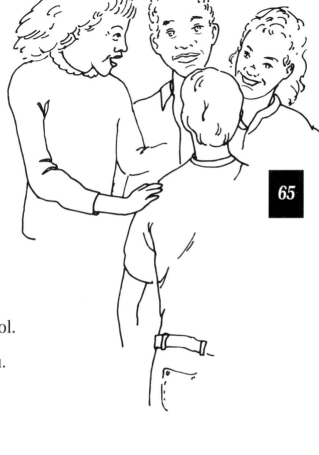

- Other kids may find out about your sexual touching problems.
- Teachers may treat you differently.
- You may have problems getting along with other kids.
- You may have to leave your school.
- Some kids may feel scared of you.

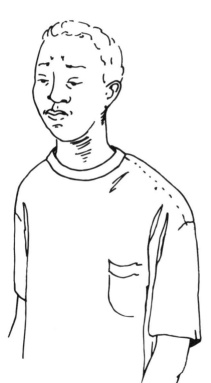

Your sexual touching problems can cause <u>TRUSTING</u> PROBLEMS:

- You may feel you can't trust others.

- Others may feel they can't trust you.

- You may feel you can't trust yourself.

66

Your sexual touching problems can cause PROBLEMS IN THE WAY
YOU THINK ABOUT YOURSELF:

- You may begin to think you are a bad person because you have committed a sexual offense.
- You may confuse bad behavior with being a bad person. You are not a bad person, even if your behavior is bad.
- You may think you have to hurt others before they hurt you.

Your sexual touching problems can cause LEGAL PROBLEMS:

- You may have to tell a judge, police officer, or caseworker what you did.
- You may have to live somewhere else and go to school somewhere else.
- You may get punished.

68

REMEMBER! Sexual offending hurts others and is against the law!

Sexual Offense Cycle

What is a <u>sexual</u> <u>offense</u> <u>cycle</u>? A sexual offense cycle is made up of the *steps* that lead to hurting someone in a sexual way or committing a sexual offense. *A sexual offense does not just happen by accident or without thinking about it.*

Kids can learn how to tell if they are having thoughts, feelings, or behaviors that might lead to doing a sexual offense.

72

It is important to learn this so that you can **STOP** yourself before you hurt someone else.

Some kids have a hard time admitting that they planned their sexual offenses. Most of the time, kids *think* about what they are going to do *before* they do it.

Most sexual offenses are done in secret.

This is because the person knows what he or she is doing is wrong, and that he or she will get in trouble if anyone finds out.

74

It takes planning to get the person you want to do sexual things with alone!

The way we learn to **STOP** sexual offenses is to:

figure out when we are about to act out sexually

and

practice ways to **STOP** that from happening.

This keeps us from hurting others and from hurting ourselves.

Let's think about it like this:

A sexual offense is like a storm, you can tell if it is going to happen. When it gets ready to storm, people go inside, the wind blows, the clouds get dark, the leaves turn over, and the thunder sounds.

When a kid gets ready to act out sexually, he or she starts having thoughts, feelings and behaviors that let the kid and others know that he or she is at risk to offend.

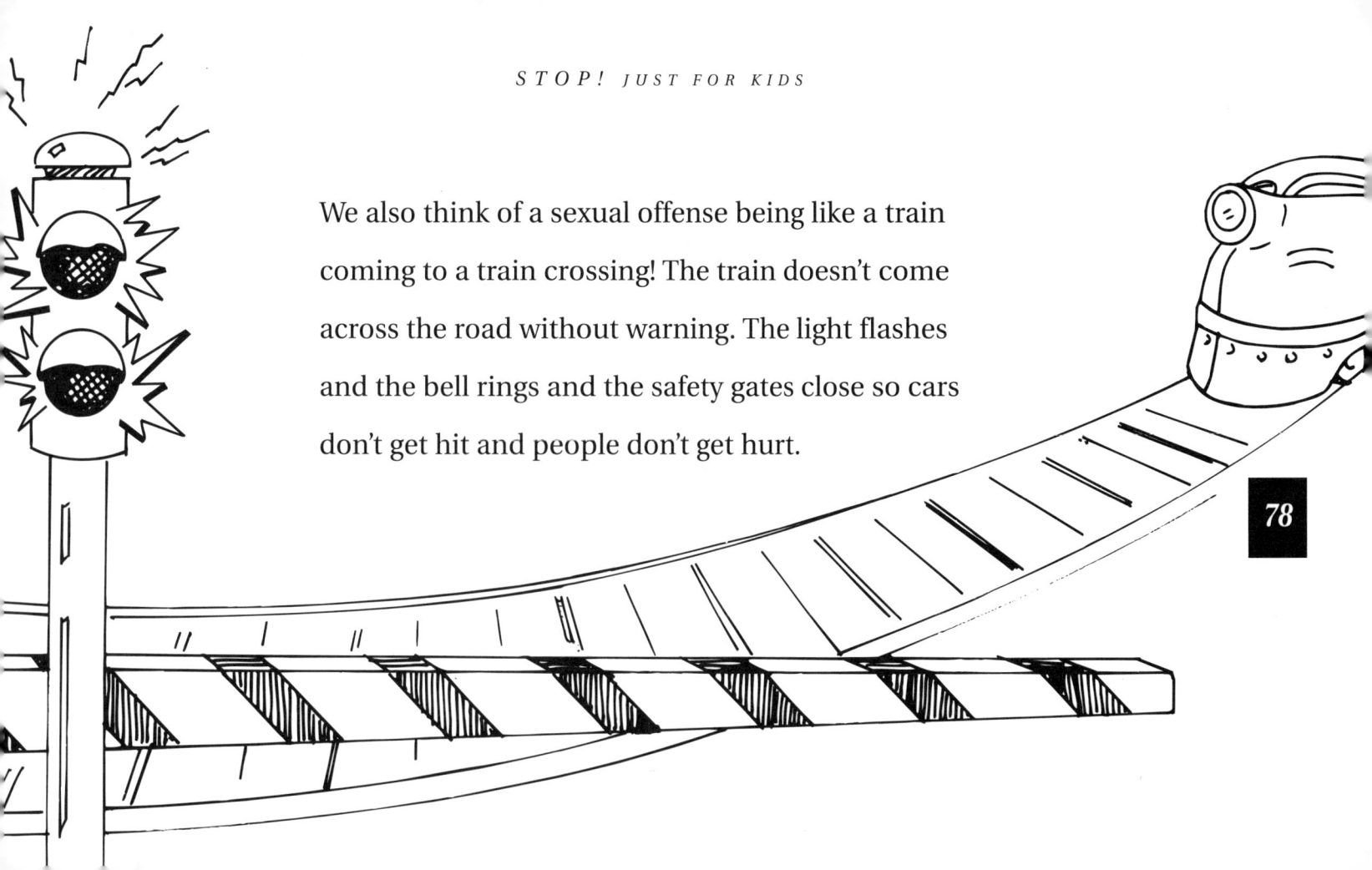

We also think of a sexual offense being like a train coming to a train crossing! The train doesn't come across the road without warning. The light flashes and the bell rings and the safety gates close so cars don't get hit and people don't get hurt.

78

Just like there are warning signs before we make the decision to sexually offend someone.

The steps that lead up to sexually offending someone are called your *sexual offense cycle.*

If kids with sexual touching problems have a sexual offense cycle, then how do they know it is getting ready to start?

What starts a sexual offense cycle? A <u>trigger</u>!

80

A trigger is something that makes a kid start thinking or feeling things that lead to wanting to touch someone sexually, or do a sexual offense.

A trigger starts their cycle.

Sometimes a trigger is a person or a certain type of clothes that remind you of when someone hurt or abused *you*.

82

Sometimes a trigger is a *feeling*, like:

      anger (if you don't get your way),

      sadness (because of a loss),

      <u>revenge</u> (to get even or get back), or

      <u>sexual</u> <u>arousal</u> (about a person or a body part).

Sometimes a trigger is a thought of what happened in your past, or what it would be like to have sex with someone. Here are some of our triggers that can make it easier for us to start an abuse cycle:

- Anger.

- Bathing suits.

- Inappropriate pictures.

- Feeling sad.

- Dark rooms.

- Invading the <u>personal</u> <u>space</u> of others.

If we can realize when a trigger is happening, then we can ...

STOP,

think,

and

make good choices.

Sometimes kids with sexual touching problems feel sexually aroused.

86

Let's talk about sexual arousal.

Sexual arousal is when you have sexual thoughts and exciting urges or tingly feelings in your private parts.

Feeling sexually aroused is OK!

Feeling sexually aroused is normal!

Sometimes kids who feel sexually aroused decide to touch their own private parts. This is called <u>masturbation</u>.

Masturbation is when kids touch their own private parts because it feels good sexually.

88

Lots of times kids have thoughts, daydreams, or images about being sexual. These are called <u>fantasies</u>.

Having safe fantasies and choosing to masturbate in a private place are normal things for kids to do.

<u>Sexuality</u> is a healthy part of every kid.

But sometimes, when kids with sexual touching problems feel sexually aroused, they think about doing *harmful* sexual things.

And sometimes sexual fantasies are not safe and can trigger your sexual offense cycle; especially when you think of doing sexual things with other kids.

90

Remember that you must have *consent* from someone who is the *right age* and *able to give permission* before you do anything sexual.

And remember that it is *not* OK to use these ways to get someone to be sexual with you:

- Playing tricks.
- Threatening people.
- Scaring people.
- Bribing people.
- Physically hurting people.

And remember that the person has to be old enough to say it is OK, and be able to understand what you are asking them to do.

92

Sometimes kids who have been sexually abused have other feelings when they are sexually aroused like sadness, anger, confusion, <u>frustration</u>, and <u>jealousy</u>.

These are feelings to talk about with your therapist, caregivers, or treatment group.

It is risky for kids with sexual touching problems to have sexual thoughts about hurting others or doing sexual things with people who can't give permission.

94

It is dangerous to masturbate about those kinds of sexual thoughts because it can start your sexual offense cycle by making you want to do sexual things with people even when they don't want to!

It is always best to be *honest* about your sexual thoughts with your therapist. Your therapist can help you learn about appropriate sexual thoughts that won't hurt you or others.

96

Remember … there is a right time and a right place to talk about sexual thoughts. It is a good idea to ask your therapist to help you decide this.

Ask yourself …

Is this the right time?

Is this the right place?

Kids with sexual touching problems sometimes decide that they want to do sexual things with someone. Lots of times they try to get other kids to do sexual things with them even though the other kids don't understand or don't want to.

This is called set-up or <u>grooming</u>.

Let's talk about GROOMING.

98

Grooming is setting others up so you can sexually offend them.

Sometimes grooming means being nice to people, so they will trust you and you can sexually offend.

This is *different* than being nice because you *care*, because in grooming your purpose is to *use someone sexually* ... for your *own pleasure* or to *hurt someone.*

Kids do a lot of different things to set up or groom their victims, like:

- Giving presents.

- Talking sexual.

- Gaining trust by being nice.

- Getting in others' personal space.

- Bribing with money or candy.

- Giving special attention.

Only you can be *honest* about your purpose.

Each kid with sexual touching problems has his or her own set of grooming behaviors.

What are some ways that you set up or groomed others?

_____

_____

_____

_____

_____

When you understand how you pick and set up a person, you will be able to teach your family or <u>support</u> <u>system</u> so they can help you be careful.

Sometimes kids act out their feelings without understanding what is happening. Other people may be able to tell that something is wrong with you by the way you are acting. This is called a <u>warning sign</u>.

104

Usually kids with sexual touching problems have feelings or behaviors, before they decide to sexually act out, that other people can see.

Only you can be completely honest about your feelings and thoughts. But until you learn how to be completely honest and really want to stop hurting others sexually, it is good to have support people who can help.

Those people can tell you when they see warning signs that you are getting ready to make bad choices.

Let's talk some more about WARNING SIGNS!

Warning signs are the things we teach ourselves and others about how to tell when we are at risk to make bad choices or do a sexual offense.

106

REMEMBER! The flashing lights and the bells at the train crossing

let you know there is danger!

Warning signs let everyone know there is danger of you sexually offending.

Here are examples of warning signs:

- Being alone a lot, and not talking to others about your feelings.

- Talking sexual to kids to test whether they would be easy to set up.

- Not being *honest* about your feelings by hiding secrets, worries or anger.

Here are some other warning signs:

- Playing with kids younger than you so that you can do sexual things with them.

- Horseplay or wrestling so that you can touch others' bodies or private parts.

- Touching others without asking.

- Feeling like you are in trouble for something you did not do! — because then you may try to play "get-back" and hurt *someone else,* since *you* are feeling hurt.

110

Kids with sexual touching problems sometimes have thoughts about hurting others sexually. Sometimes kids will believe that it is okay to do sexual things without permission or when the other person can't give permission. When kids have problems with the way they think about sexual things, they are having <u>thinking</u> <u>problems</u>.

Let's talk about THINKING PROBLEMS!

Thinking problems are one way kids tell themselves it is okay to hurt

someone sexually.

112

Thinking problems are thoughts that:

- <u>Minimize</u> what you did by acting like it's not your fault.

- Blame the person that you hurt.

- Make the details of what you did seem like no big deal.

- Pretend like your behavior really didn't hurt the other person.

- <u>Rationalize</u> or make excuses for your behavior.

- Deny what you did was wrong and that you hurt someone.

  - Deny you are responsible for hurting someone.

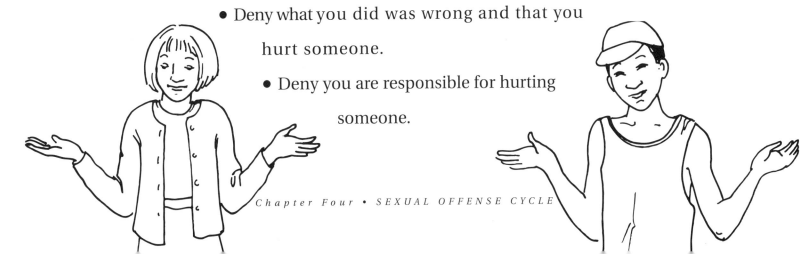

Examples of thinking problems are:

"I *really* didn't *hurt* anyone."

"He *deserves* to be hurt — because *I* was hurt too!"

"She *wanted* to have sex with me *because she was nice to me!*"

Can you list some thinking problems that you have?

114

_____

_____

_____

_____

So remember, hurting another person sexually doesn't just happen by accident. Most kids have thoughts, feelings or behaviors that can warn them and others that they need help and positive attention. When you understand what makes you have urges to do hurtful things, then you are on your way to being able to **STOP** doing those things.

Now we understand how we hurt others sexually and how we sexually offend.

It is time to learn how to make choices to STOP hurting others.

116

Next, let's talk about BLOCKS!

Blocks are barriers or walls that **STOP** something from happening.

There are two kinds of blocks:

<u>outside</u> blocks

and

<u>inside</u> <u>blocks</u>.

Outside blocks are a pretend wall you or your support system put up *outside of you,* to help you **STOP** your sexual offense cycle.

118

Examples of outside blocks are:

- Not being alone with smaller children.

- Having adults watch and supervise you.

- Spending time with friends that are your age.

- Having someone tell you that you are showing warning signs.

Inside blocks are a pretend wall that you build *inside of you,* to help you remember to make good choices and **STOP** your sexual offense cycle.

120

Inside blocks are in your heart and in your head.

They remind you not to sexually offend others.

Examples of inside blocks are:

- Knowing what will start your sexual offense cycle and watching out for it.
- Caring about what your behavior does to others.
- Knowing the law and the consequences of breaking the law.
- Knowing how to make good choices.
- Knowing how to get out of your sexual offense cycle.

Can you list some ways you could use outside or inside blocks to help STOP your sexual offense cycle?

(OUTSIDE BLOCK EXAMPLE: My mother knows that it isn't safe for me to be around little kids, especially when I am angry. INSIDE BLOCK EXAMPLE: When I think about how much my behavior hurt the kid I did sexual things to, it makes me not want to do it again.)

122

_____

_____

_____

123

Another way to keep you from sexually offending is to think about *why* you should not sexually offend. Here are some of the reasons we choose *not* to re-offend.

- You hurt others and yourself.
- You could have to leave your family.
- You could get a <u>sexually</u> <u>transmitted</u> <u>disease</u>.
- You could go to jail.
- You could ruin someone's life.
- It is wrong.

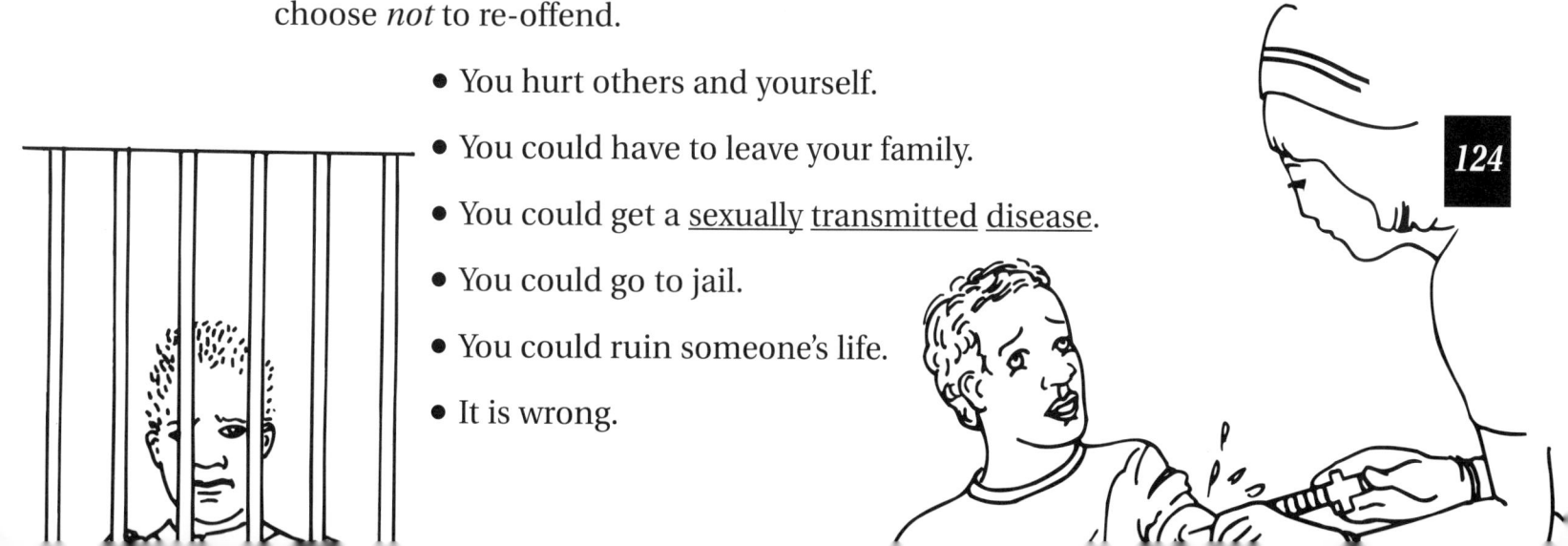

124

The best way to learn how to **STOP** hurting others is to …

be *honest,*

practice *caring* about others,

and

listen to your therapist!

Making Good Choices

NOW THAT WE understand the harmful choices we have made, it is time to learn how to make healthy and safe choices.

All of us have a best friend to help us make good choices. This best friend is our <u>conscience</u>.

A conscience is a voice inside of you that tells you what is right or what is wrong and how to make good choices.

It may help to think of your conscience as a good animal that lives inside of you and helps you make good decisions.

Can you think of your good animal? Draw it here.

Part of making good choices is learning to respect others. Respect means to think about and care about how others feel.

Can you list some people you respect?

_____

_____

_____

_____

Kids who have a lot of respect for others develop something that is called <u>empathy</u>.

Empathy means you know and understand in your head (thoughts), and in your heart (feelings) how someone else feels.

132

It is a kind of caring about others that helps to remind us to make *good* choices and *not hurt* others.

Kids who have respect and empathy for others:

- Help each other.

- Do activities together (like going to the movies).

- Trust each other to talk about feelings.

- Take turns.

- Do nice things for each other.

- Forgive each other for mistakes.

There are lots of things that you can do to help you make good choices.

You can:

- Try to get <u>positive</u> <u>attention</u>.
- Learn to <u>problem</u> <u>solve</u>.
- Be <u>assertive</u>.
- Talk about your feelings.

Positive attention is the attention you get for good behavior.

An example of good behavior is following directions.

Another example is saying, "Thank you."

What are some ways that you can get positive attention?

_____

_____

_____

_____

_____

_____

_____

136

Positive attention is when people pay attention to you in a way that makes you *feel safe and that you are a good person.*

Positive attention is getting noticed for all the *good things* you do.

137

You can get positive attention by:

- Asking for it!
- Being respectful!
- Being friendly!
- Doing your school work!
- Being honest!
- Being nice!
- Cleaning your room!

138

Another way to make good choices is to practice problem solving.

First you have to realize that there is a problem. Like when you are playing kickball and you don't get your turn and you get mad. You could make a good choice and try to solve the problem instead of yelling, screaming and throwing a temper tantrum.

Let's say some more about PROBLEM SOLVING!

Problem solving has four steps.

    1. What is the problem?

    2. What are some different answers or ways to *solve* the problem?

    3. Pick the way that seems best and see how it works.

    4. Was it a good answer that didn't hurt anyone?

140

4 — What happened? Was anyone hurt? Was this a GOOD answer?

3 — What seems to be the BEST thing to do?

2 — What are some things I can do to solve the problem?

1 — What is the problem?

Chapter Five • MAKING GOOD CHOICES

REMEMBER! For problem solving to work, you must:

- Be positive! This means to expect good things to happen.
- Be patient! This means be willing to wait for the good things.
- Be respectful! This means to think and care about others.

142

Problem solving helps you see the choices and get along with people.

It is *easier* to solve problems when you are *assertive*.

So … let's say something about ASSERTIVE!

144

Being assertive means to stand up for yourself and tell how you feel or what you want without hurting anyone.

Being assertive helps you tell about your feelings in a positive way.

146

One way to be assertive is to stand up straight, look someone in the eye, take a deep breath, talk slowly and clearly in a calm voice, and *say* what it is you want.

Another way to make good choices is to *talk about* your feelings.

148

We have already learned about what feelings are. But it is very important to *talk* about your feelings *instead of acting them out.* Can you think of some reasons why talking about your feelings is making a good choice?

Sharing your feelings is a good choice because it lets others know what you want and how you feel.

150

Sharing your feelings might help others to talk about their feelings, too.

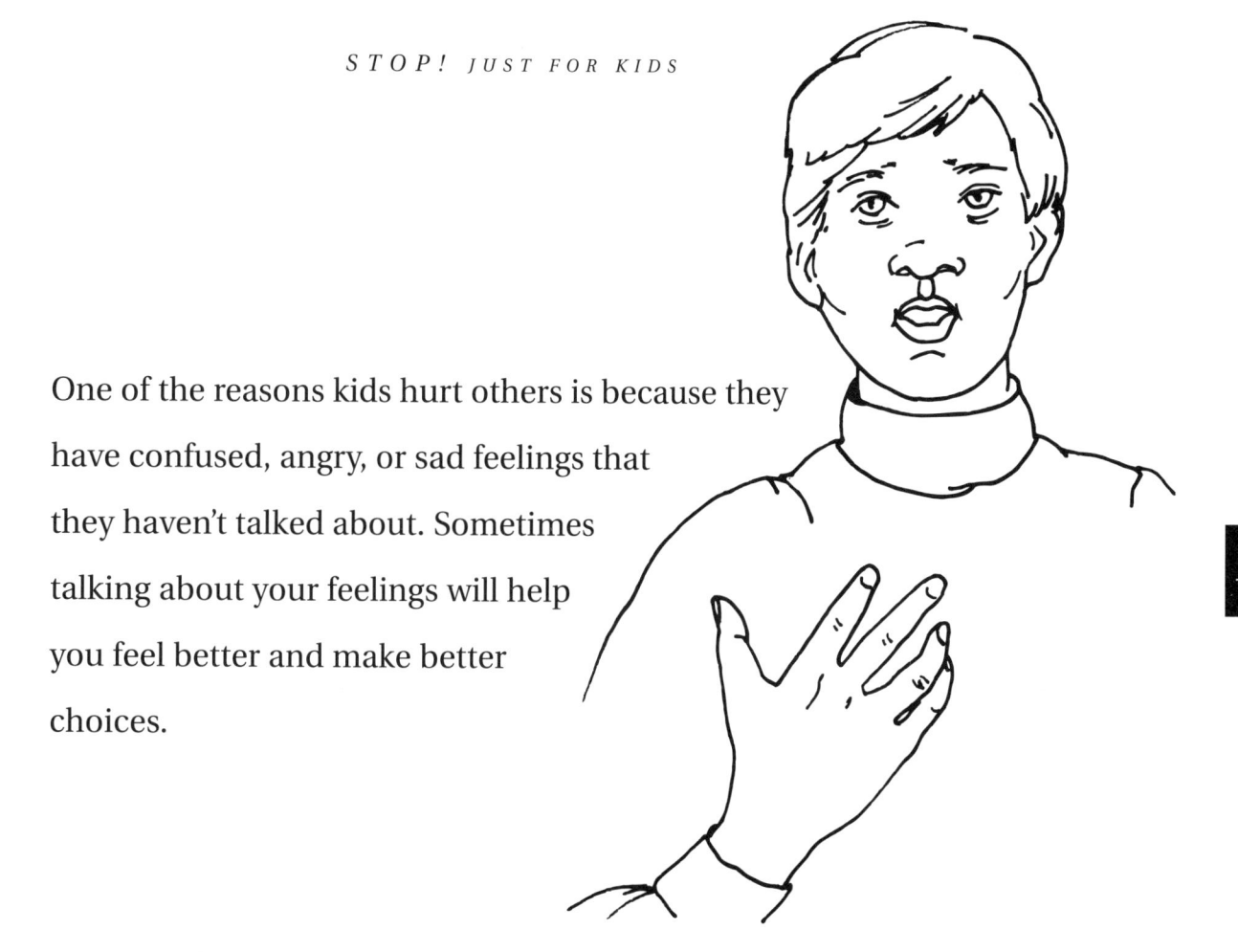

One of the reasons kids hurt others is because they
have confused, angry, or sad feelings that
they haven't talked about. Sometimes
talking about your feelings will help
you feel better and make better
choices.

152

It is better to talk it out than act it out!

154

A FEW LAST WORDS

Now we have come to the end of our book. Remember that honesty is very important. Your therapist and family won't know how to help if you don't tell the truth.

It is *especially* important to tell your bad, sad, and mad feelings to someone else so that you don't turn them into hurting others.

Sexual offending hurts others and is illegal. So remember ... you can make good choices to respect others and **STOP** sexually offending.

156

Thank you for reading our book, and good luck!

The Good News Bears

158

ABOUT TERRI ALLRED AND GARY BURNS

Terri Allred, M.T.S. is an experienced counselor, educator, and national lecturer in the field of sexual violence. She is currently the Program Coordinator for the Columbus (Ohio) Area Rape Treatment Program. Gary Burns, M.S. has many years experience as an educator working with troubled children and is the Director of Education for Hermitage Hall Residential Treatment Program for sexual offenders in Nashville, Tennessee. He has lectured nationally with Allred at such conferences as the National Symposium on Child Sexual Abuse and the National Training Conference of the Adolescent Perpetrator Network.

Terri Allred and Gary Burns worked together at Hermitage Hall with the young authors of *Stop! Just for Kids* and revised the original manuscript for the purpose of publishing. This book is meant to be both a resource to help children understand their sexual touching problems in a therapeutic context and a springboard for individual treatment efforts on behalf of the special youngsters for whom it was published.

SELECT SAFER SOCIETY PUBLICATIONS

Roadmaps to Recovery: A Guided Workbook for Young People in Treatment by Timothy J. Kahn (1999). $20.

The Secret: Art & Healing from Sexual Abuse by Francie Lyshak (1999). $20.

Outside Looking In: When Someone You Love Is in Therapy by Patrice Moulton and Lin Harper (1999). $20.

Web of Meaning: A Developmental-Contextual Approach in Sexual Abuse Treatment by Gail Ryan & Associates (1999). $22.

Feeling Good Again by Burt Wasserman (1999). A treatment workbook for boys and girls ages 6 and up who have been sexually abused. $16.

Feeling Good Again Guide for Parents & Therapists by Burt Wasserman (1999). $8.

Female Sexual Abusers: Three Views by Patricia Davin, Ph.D., Teresa Dunbar, Ph.D., & Julia Hislop, Ph.D. (1999). $22.

Cultural Diversity in Sexual Abuser Treatment: Issues and Approaches edited by Alvin Lewis, Ph.D. (1999). $22.

Sexual Abuse in America: Epidemic of the 21st Century by Robert E. Freeman-Longo & Geral T. Blanchard (1998). $20.

Personal Sentence Completion Inventory by L.C. Miccio-Fonseca, Ph.D. (1998). $50, includes ten inventories and user's guide.

When You Don't Know Who to Call: A Consumer's Guide to Selecting Mental Health Care by Nancy Schaufele & Donna Kennedy (1998). $15.

Tell It Like It Is: A Resource for Youth in Treatment by Alice Tallmadge with Galyn Forster (1998). $15.

Assessing Sexual Abuse: A Resource Guide for Practitioners edited by Robert Prentky and Stacey Bird Edmunds (1997). $20.

Impact: Working with Sexual Abusers edited by Stacey Bird Edmunds (1997). $15.

Supervision of the Sex Offender by Georgia Cumming and Maureen Buell (1997). $25.

Shining Through: Pulling It Together After Sexual Abuse by Mindy Loiselle & Leslie Bailey Wright (1997). $12.00. (A workbook especially for girls ages 10 and up.) *Revised edition includes sections on sexuality, self-esteem, and body image.*

A Primer on the Complexities of Traumatic Memories of Childhood Sexual Abuse: A Psychobiological Approach by Fay Honey Knopp & Anna Rose Benson (1997) $25.

The Last Secret: Daughters Sexually Abused by Mothers by Bobbie Rosencrans (1997).

37 to One: Living as an Integrated Multiple by Phoenix J. Hocking (1996). $12.00.

The Brother / Sister Hurt: Recognizing the Effects of Sibling Abuse by Vernon Wiehe, PhD (1996) $10.00.

When Children Abuse: Group Treatment Strategies for Children with Impulse Control Problems by Carolyn Cunningham and Kee MacFarlane. *Incorporates and updates their well-respected previous volume **When Children Molest Children,** adding new material on medications, shame and entitlement, firesetting, and animal abuse.* (1996). $28.00.

Adult Sex Offender Assessment Packet by Mark Carich & Donya Adkerson (1995). $8.00.

The Difficult Connection: The Therapeutic Relationship in Sex Offender Treatment by Geral T. Blanchard (1995). $10.00.

From Trauma to Understanding: A Guide for Parents of Children with Sexual Behavior Problems by William D. Pithers, Alison S. Gray, Carolyn Cunningham, & Sandy Lane (1993). $5.00.

Adolescent Sexual Offender Assessment Packet by Alison Stickrod Gray & Randy Wallace (1992). $8.00.

The Relapse Prevention Workbook for Youth in Treatment by Charlene Steen (1993). $15.00.

Pathways: A Guided Workbook for Youth Beginning Treatment by Timothy J. Kahn (1990; revised 1992; 3rd printing). $15.00.

Pathways Guide for Parents of Youth Beginning Treatment by Timothy J. Kahn (1990). $7.50.

Man-to-Man, When Your Partner Says NO: Pressured Sex & Date Rape by Scott Allen Johnson (1992). $6.50.

When Your Wife Says No: Forced Sex in Marriage by Fay Honey Knopp (1994). $7.00.

Adults Molested As Children: A Survivor's Manual for Women & Men by Euan Bear with Peter Dimock (1988; 4th printing). $12.95.

Family Fallout: A Handbook for Families of Adult Sexual Abuse Survivors by Dorothy Beaulieu Landry, Med. (1991). $12.95.

Embodying Healing: Integrating Bodywork and Psychotherapy in Recovery from Childhood Sexual Abuse by Robert J. Timms, PhD, and Patrick Connors, CMT. (1992). $15.00.

The Safer Society Press publishes additional books, audiocassetttes, and training videos related to the treatment of sexual abuse.

For a catalog of our complete listings, please check the box on the order form (next page).

Order Form

Date: _____

All books shipped via United Parcel Services. Please include a street location for shipping as we can not ship to a Post Office box.

Shipping Address:

Name and/or Agency _____

Street Address (no P.O. Box) _____

City _____ State _____ Zip _____

Billing Address (if different from shipping address):

Address _____

City _____ State _____ Zip _____

Daytime Phone (____) _____ P.O. # _____

Visa or MasterCard # _____ Exp. Date _____

Signature (FOR CREDIT CARD ORDER) _____

❑ Please send me a catalog.   ❑ Do not add me to your mailing list.

Qty	Title	Unit Price	Total Cost
		Subtotal	
		VT Residents add sales tax	
		Shipping (see below)	
		Total	

Shipping & Handling

1-5 items	$5	26-30 items	$18
6-10 items	$8	31-35 items	$22
11-15 items	$10	36-40 items	$25
16-20 items	$12	41-50 items	$30
21-25 items	$15	51 + items	$35

Call for quote on rush orders

All orders must be prepaid.

Make checks payable to: SAFER SOCIETY PRESS.

All prices subject to change without notice. No Returns.

Bulk discounts available, please inquire.

Mail to:

SaferSocietyPress

PO Box 340 • Brandon, VT 05733-0340

Phone orders accepted with MasterCard or Visa

Call (802) 247-3132

MasterCard   VISA